雙語教學無敵通

Jeff Wen & Arthur McCambridge

雙語教學無敵通

Written by Jeff Wen & Arthur McCambridge
Publisher: Tony Chen
General Manager: Virginia Li
Art Editor: Jill Wu
Illustrator: Tank Chien

Rm, 4A10, 4F., No.5, Sec. 5, Xinyi Rd., Xinyi Dist.,
Taipei City 110, Taiwan.
& Rm, 7F-1, No.239, Sec. 2, Taiwan Blvd., West Dist.,
Taichung City 403, Taiwan.
TEL: 886-4-23219185

ISBN: 978-986-95445-6-6

Printed in Taiwan

MP3 Download
https://s.yam.com/TC2MO

資源下載:每頁考題 ，中文
翻譯，單字及例句，海報

英閱音躍研創
@readbig

請開啓點讀筆後點讀書封的 圖示，
開始進行點讀

Table of Contents

A Greeting

 B Connecting

1. Good afternoon, class.

2. Good day, students.

3. Good morning, everybody.

4. Hello there, Virginia.

5. Hello, everyone.

6. What a lovely day.

1. Are you feeling better today, Tony?

2. Did you sleep well?

3. Do you feel refreshed this morning?

4. How are things with you?

5. How are you doing?

6. How are you today?

7. How is it going?

8. Is everyone well?

C Introduction

1. I have five lessons with you each week.

2. I'll be teaching you English this year.

3. If you forget my name, call me sir / ma'am / miss.

4. My name is Mr. / Mrs. / Ms. Kim. I'm your new English teacher.

5. We will see each other every morning.

6. You can call me Mr. Kim.

D Roll Call

1. Does anyone know where Peter is?

2. Say "yes" when I call your name.

3. What's the matter with Chris today?

4. What's wrong with Stanley today?

5. Who is absent today?

6. Who isn't here today?

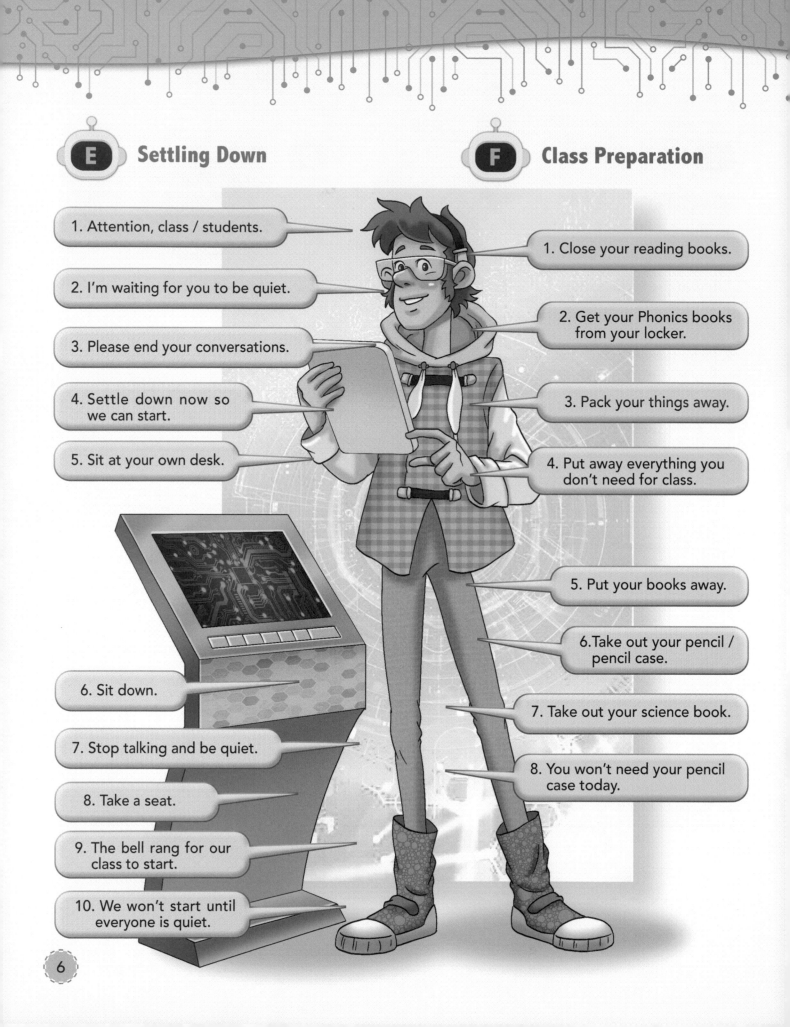

E Settling Down

1. Attention, class / students.

2. I'm waiting for you to be quiet.

3. Please end your conversations.

4. Settle down now so we can start.

5. Sit at your own desk.

6. Sit down.

7. Stop talking and be quiet.

8. Take a seat.

9. The bell rang for our class to start.

10. We won't start until everyone is quiet.

F Class Preparation

1. Close your reading books.

2. Get your Phonics books from your locker.

3. Pack your things away.

4. Put away everything you don't need for class.

5. Put your books away.

6. Take out your pencil / pencil case.

7. Take out your science book.

8. You won't need your pencil case today.

G Starting the Lesson

1. I hope you are all ready for your English lesson.

2. I think we can start now.

3. Is everybody ready to start?

4. Let's begin our lesson now.

5. Let's continue where we left off yesterday.

6. Let's look at the presentation I prepared for you.

7. Let's start on Unit 4.

8. Listen to the conversation.

9. Look at the screen.

10. Now we can get down to work.

11. Open your books to page 25.

12. Pay attention as I will ask questions afterwards.

H Dealing with Lateness

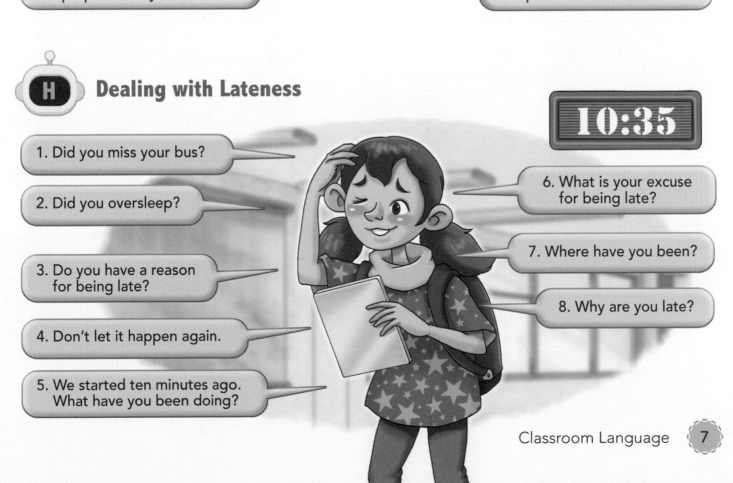

10:35

1. Did you miss your bus?

2. Did you oversleep?

3. Do you have a reason for being late?

4. Don't let it happen again.

5. We started ten minutes ago. What have you been doing?

6. What is your excuse for being late?

7. Where have you been?

8. Why are you late?

Dialogue I

Teacher: Please put away your toy, Andrew.

Student: It is not a toy - it is my sharpener.

Teacher: If you play with it, it is a toy. Put it away and follow in your book.

Student: Peter is playing with his marker!

Teacher: Class, please do not play with your stationery. We will have a quiz at the end of the period, so please pay attention.

Student: Yes, Mr. Kim.

Dialogue II

Student: I am sorry I am late, Mr. Kim.

Teacher: Claire, this is the second time this week.

Student: It is not my fault. My little brother got up late. Then he could not find his pencil case.

Teacher: And that took you 30 minutes?

Student: No, we found it quickly. But we missed the bus.

Teacher: Maybe you should wake your brother when you get up from now on.

Student: OK. I will wake up my brother from now on.

Teacher: Great idea. Please sit down at your desk and take out your workbook.

Student: Yes, sir.

Unit 2

Simple Instructions During Lessons

 A Basic Instructions

 B Useful Instructions

A Basic Instructions

1. Come in.
2. Come to the front of the class.
3. Go out.
4. Hold your books / pens up.
5. Put your hands down.
6. Put your hands up.
7. Show me your pencil.
8. Sit down.
9. Stand by your desk.
10. Stand up.

B Useful Instructions

1. Again, please.
2. Listen to this audio.
3. Look at Activity Five.
4. Open your books to page…
5. Repeat after me.
6. Turn to page…
7. We'll learn how to write a capital C today.
8. Who's next?
9. You have five minutes to do this.
10. You need a pencil / an eraser.

C Comprehension Check

1. Are you ready to begin?

2. Are you with me?

3. Can you do it by yourself now?

4. Do you follow me?

5. Do you get it?

6. Do you know what I mean?

7. Do you understand?

8. Good so far?

9. I don't get it.

10. I don't understand.

11. Is it clear?

12. Like this?

13. One more time, please.

14. Say it again, please.

15. What did you say?

D Wrapping up the Lesson

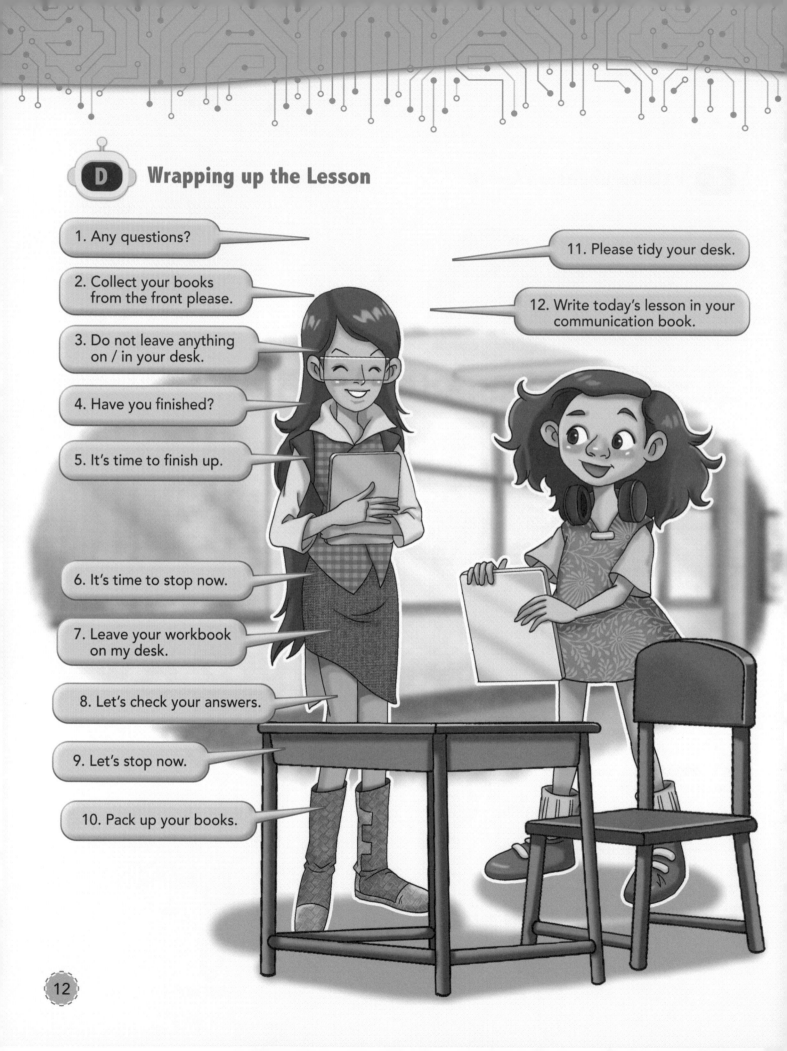

1. Any questions?

2. Collect your books from the front please.

3. Do not leave anything on / in your desk.

4. Have you finished?

5. It's time to finish up.

6. It's time to stop now.

7. Leave your workbook on my desk.

8. Let's check your answers.

9. Let's stop now.

10. Pack up your books.

11. Please tidy your desk.

12. Write today's lesson in your communication book.

E Group Work

1. Choose a person to tell the class about your decision.

2. Choose a team leader.

3. Divide the work among your group.

4. Give every team member a job to do.

5. Name your team.

6. Nominate a leader.

7. Pair up.

8. Team up in groups of four.

9. Work together in groups of three.

10. Work with your partner.

F Sequence Words

1. After that

2. All in all

3. Finally

4. First / In the beginning

5. Following that

6. In conclusion

7. Next / Second

8. Third / Then

Dialogue I

Teacher: You will need a pencil and an eraser today.

Student: Are we going to draw a picture?

Teacher: No. We will complete some questions in the book. Now open your textbook to page 31.

Student: I finished page 31 at home.

Teacher: Good work. For the rest of you, work with your neighbor to complete the simple questions on page 31.

Student: What does daily mean?

Teacher: Daily means every day. Write down something you do every day.

Student: I come to school every day.

Teacher: You are right.

Dialogue II

Teacher: For today's project you will need to form teams of three.

Student: Can we make a team of four?

Teacher: There are 9 students in class, and I would like to have three teams, so please stick to three per group.

Student: Okay. We have three members already.

Teacher: Now, choose a name for your team.

Student: Can we choose any name?

Teacher: Only names that are not rude. That means you have to choose a nice name.

Student: Our team's name is Super Smart.

Teacher: You will have to choose a team leader to write the team's name on the board.

Student: Brian is our leader.

A Ending the Lesson

1. Finish with what you are doing.

2. I'm afraid it's time to finish now.

3. It's almost time to stop.

4. That's all for today. You can go now.

5. There's the bell. It's time to stop.

6. We'll have to stop here.

B With Time to Spare at the End of the Lesson

1. Read quietly until the end of class.

2. Sit quietly until the bell goes.

3. The bell hasn't rung yet.

4. The lesson doesn't finish until ten thirty.

5. There are still five minutes to go.

6. There is a couple of minutes. You can start with homework.

7. We have an extra ten minutes.

8. We seem to have finished early.

9. We still have a couple of minutes left.

10. Your watch must be fast.

C — Last-Minute Reminders

1. Back to your places.

2. Hang on a moment.

3. Just a moment, please.

4. Just hold on a second.

5. One more thing before you go.

6. Stay in your seats until I have handed out the papers.

7. Stay seated until after the announcement.

8. Stay where you are for a bit.

9. Wait a minute.

D — Ending and Scheduling the Lesson

1. Let's resume the reading tomorrow.

2. Let's take a break and continue after recess.

3. That's enough for today. We'll carry on next time.

4. We'll continue in the next period.

5. We'll continue this chapter next Monday.

6. We'll do the rest of this chapter next time.

7. We'll finish this exercise in the next lesson.

8. We'll start from here when I see you again.

Assigning Homework

 Saying Goodbye

1. Do exercise B on page 7 for your homework.

The worksheet is homework.

2. Don't forget to bring your color pens tomorrow.

3. Please complete the homework on page 24 in your workbook.

4. Preview the next unit for Tuesday.

5. Remember to complete your homework.

6. Remember to finish your homework on page 15.

7. Study the rest of the reading by yourselves.

8. The worksheet is homework.

9. There is no homework today.

10. This is your homework for today.

11. You can continue with your work tomorrow.

12. You can find the answers to your homework in the unit we did today.

1. Enjoy your short holiday.

2. Goodbye, everyone.

3. Have a good vacation.

4. Have a wonderful weekend.

5. See you again next Friday.

6. See you in the computer lab after the break.

7. See you next time.

8. See you tomorrow morning.

9. Take care.

10. Until tomorrow.

G Leaving the Room

1. Don't leave any books on your desk when you go home.

2. Everybody, line up outside.

3. Form a line and wait for the bell.

4. Get into line.

5. Hurry up and make two lines in front of the classroom.

6. Leave silently. Other classes are still working.

7. Let's leave row by row.

8. Look around your desk and pick up any trash.

9. Make sure there is nothing in your desk.

10. Remember to let your parents sign the communication book.

11. Take all food out of your locker before you go home.

12. Take your lunch bag home and remember to wash your lunch box.

13. Try not to make any noise while you are leaving.

14. Walk in single file to the computer lab.

Dialogue I

Teacher: You have about ten minutes to finish the project.

Student: That is not enough time.

Teacher: Do as much as you can in the meantime.

Student: Will we continue tomorrow?

Teacher: If we finish our work early tomorrow, I will give you some more time to work on the project.

Student: Do we have any homework?

Teacher: Yes, I will write it on the board. Please copy it into your communication book.

Student: I am done.

Teacher: Please bring your communication book to the front, so I can sign it.

Student: I am first.

Teacher: Please make a line and don't push.

Dialogue II

Teacher: Before you leave, please check around your desk for any trash.

Student: Someone threw candy wrappers on the floor.

Teacher: Be a nice student and pick it up for us.

Student: Okay.

Teacher: Let's leave row by row. Row one, please stand up and exit the classroom quietly.

Student: Yes, sir.

Teacher: Don't forget your lunch bags. I see some hanging on the desks.

Student: Thank you. My mom will be angry if I forget it at school.

Teacher: Goodbye everyone.

Student: Have a good weekend, sir.

Teacher: Thank you. See you next Monday.

A **Getting Students' Attention with Call-and-Response Phrases**

Teacher	Student
1. All set	You bet!
2. And a hush fell across the room!	Shhh!
3. Are you ready, kids?	Aye, aye, Captain!
4. Attention!	One, two!
5. Banana	Split!
6. Crystal	Clear!
7. Eeny meeny	Miny mo!
8. Flat tire	Shhh!
9. Goodness Gracious!	Great balls of fire!
10. Hakuna	Matata!
11. Hands in the air	Like you just don't care!
12. Hands on top	Everybody stop!
13. Here I come to save the day	Mighty Mouse is on his way!
14. Hocus pocus	Time to focus!
15. Hocus pocus	Everybody focus!
16. Holy moly	Guacamole!
17. I am on a quest	To be my best!
18. If you can't make a mistake	You can't make anything!
19. Macaroni and cheese	Everybody freeze!
20. Marco	Polo!

Teacher	Student
21. Meanwhile	Back at the ranch!
22. Mona	Lisa!
23. No bees, no honey	No work, no money!
24. Oh me	Oh my!
25. One, two!	Eyes on you!
26. One, two, eyes on me	One, two, eyes on you!
27. Piece of pie	Piece of cake!
28. Ready Set	You bet!
29. Ready to rock	Ready to roll!
30. Scooby Dooby Doo	Where are you?
31. Sponge Bob	Square Pants!
32. To infinity	And beyond!
33. We are learning	All the time!
34. What are we here for?	To learn!
35. When the hand goes up	The mouth goes shut!
36. When we listen	We learn!
37. Who lives in a pineapple under the sea?	SpongeBob Squarepants!
38. Who loves you?	You do!
39. Work hard	Do right!
40. You snooze	You lose!
41. Zip, zip, zap	We're all that!

B Saying No in a Child-Friendly Way

1. A safer choice would be to use scissors.

2. As soon as we have watched the video, we can start homework.

3. First write your sentences, then draw a picture.

4. Help me understand.

5. I need you to listen to the song.

6. I'll consider it.

7. I'm all done talking about playing a game.

8. I'm not talking about that.

9. I'm wondering if blue won't be better.

10. Is that how we use a pencil?

11. It's time to open our math books.

12. Let me think about that.

13. Let's be safe by putting the scissors away.

14. Let's talk about what is an option.

15. Let's try that a different way.

16. Our agreement was that you fill up your water bottle during recess.

17. That's not a choice right now.

18. That's not your choice.

19. The expectation is that you finish before the end of class.

20. We already talked about using a red pen.

21. We can't watch a video right now, but we can sing together.

22. What I should hear is a conversation about butterflies.

23. You already asked to change seats.

24. You can choose to finish now or finish in break time.

25. You have my answer.

26. Your job is to write a poem right now.

Expressing Warning

1. Be careful.

2. Better safe than sorry.

3. Beware of the steps.

4. Don't do that!

5. I don't think you should eat that.

6. I have to warn you that homework is due tomorrow morning.

7. I highly recommend you not to waste time.

8. I warn you not to sit on the table.

9. I'm warning you: If you do that again, I will have to call your parents.

10. If I were you, I would not use a cutter.

11. If you play with your pencil, it becomes a toy.

12. If you talk during class, you will miss the instructions.

13. Keep away from the balcony.

14. Pay attention when you are using scissors.

15. Please, do not eat in class.

16. Watch out!

17. You must not break the rules.

18. You should not bring a pet to school.

Dialogue I

Teacher: Who lives in a pineapple under the sea?

Student: SpongeBob Squarepants!

Teacher: Now that I have your attention. Let's focus on the picture on the screen.

Student: Is it a mouse?

Teacher: Almost. Any guesses.

Student: It looks like a big mouse. Is it a rat?

Teacher: No. It is actually a squirrel.

Student: There are some squirrels in the park close to my house.

Teacher: Yes, they are commonly seen in city parks.

Student: I have a cat at home.

Teacher: That's wonderful. As soon as we are done with today's lesson about squirrels, we'll talk about cats.

Student: Okay.

Teacher: I want everyone to draw a squirrel in a tree in your workbook.

Student: I am going to draw my cat.

Teacher: That's not a choice right now. Please follow my instructions.

Dialogue II

Teacher: Jenny, please put away your exacto knife. It is not a toy.

Student: Can I put it on my desk?

Teacher: A safer choice would be to put it in your book bag.

Student: I need it for art class.

Teacher: This is not art class.

Student: But ….

Teacher: I am done talking about that.

Student: It won't hurt anyone.

Teacher: If you do not put it away, I will have to write a note to you parents.

Student: I am sorry, Miss Kim. I will put it away.

Teacher: Thank you, Jenny.

Unit 5

Advice and Suggestions

A Asking Advice from the Teacher

1. Could you help me choose the book?

2. Do you think I should take the test now?

3. If you were me, what would you do?

4. Should I apply for the leadership camp?

5. What brand do you recommend I buy?

6. What do you advise me to do?

7. What do you suggest?

8. What do you think I should do?

9. What ought I to do?

10. What should I do?

11. Which is better?

B Advising the Student Against Something

1. If I were you, I wouldn't sit on the desk.

2. It is a bad idea to give up on learning English.

3. It is against school rules to eat in class.

4. It is dangerous to play with your scissors during class.

5. It is not a good idea to skip class.

6. It is not acceptable to chew with an open mouth.

7. It is not right to take your classmate's pen.

8. It is not wise to remove your facemask when you are sick.

9. It will be a mistake to cheat on your exam.

10. It would be a waste of time to play video games before a test.

11. One thing you should not do, is pick your nose.

C Giving Suggestions

1. Have you thought about using a highlighter?

2. Have you tried to find more information on the Net?

3. I think your only option is to talk to your teacher directly.

4. If I were in your shoes [position], I would join the team.

5. If I were you, I would discuss it with my parents.

6. It might be a good solution to let a friend read it first.

7. It would probably be better [safer / wiser] to do every assignment.

8. It's generally a good idea to review your answers before handing it in.

9. My advice would be to take a mock test before the exam.

10. One thing you could do is practice your speech on a friend.

11. The sooner you call [write / confirm / cancel], the better.

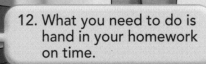

12. What you need to do is hand in your homework on time.

13. Why don't you study with a friend?

14. You could always come talk to me during recess.

15. You had better go to the restroom before class.

16. You should go to bed before ten.

17. Your only option is to take the test again.

D Responding to Advice

Accepting Advice

1. I never thought of that.

2. I think you're right - I'll do that!

3. I'll give it a try and see what happens.

4. That's a good idea!

5. Yes, that might help.

Rejecting Advice

1. I don't think that would help.

2. I don't think that's the solution, but thanks anyway.

3. I'm not convinced of that, but I'll think about it.

4. I've already tried that but thank you for the suggestion.

5. No. I don't think so.

Dialogue I

Student: Can I write with a pen?

Teacher: I would advise you to use a pencil.

Student: Why?

Teacher: If you write your work in pencil, you can erase any mistakes.

Student: Oh yeah! And it would also look neat.

Teacher: That's right. A good option is also to use a mechanical pencil, so you don't have to sharpen it.

Student: My mom told me the same. She bought me this pencil.

Teacher: Good. Now finish your writing.

Student: I'm almost done. Can I hand it in now?

Teacher: It is always best to review your writing before submitting it.

Student: Okay.

Dialogue II

Student: There is so much information in our book. I don't know what to study.

Teacher: Have you thought about highlighting the important facts while reading?

Student: I started doing it but forgot to keep doing it.

Teacher: It is generally a good idea to make it a habit.

Student: The only habit I have is playing online games before going to bed.

Teacher: If I were you, I would only play online games over the weekend.

Student: Do you think I should study in the morning or afternoon?

Teacher: Researchers suggest that younger students study in the morning.

Student: My mother also forces me to study on Saturday mornings.

Teacher: It seems that studying in the morning is your only option.

A Starting the Discussion

1. Could I ask about your camping weekend?

2. Could you tell me the meaning of this word?

3. Do you happen to know what the new student's name is?

4. Do you happen to know whether or not the bookshop is open?

5. Do you know if Steven is sick?

6. Do you know what kind of insect this is?

7. I'd like to know about the book you read.

8. I'm interested in the picture you drew.

9. What are the advantages and disadvantages of walking to school?

10. What do you think are the causes of global warming?

11. What do you think is the problem between Mary and Carina?

12. What do you think is the problem with the cafeteria?

13. What do you think of our new textbook?

B Giving Answers and Opinions

1. I (strongly) believe that screen time should be limited.

2. I definitely think that breakfast is important.

3. I have reason to believe that you will pass the test in flying colors.

4. I strongly believe in the power of education.

5. I'm (very) sure that your mother will approve.

6. In my opinion, fast food is not healthy.

7. In my reckoning, our history teacher is knowledgeable.

8. In my view, many students do not sleep enough.

9. Well, I think kids should do more sports.

10. Well, if you ask me, homework should be reduced.

C Agreeing with One Strong Word

1. Absolutely!

2. Agree.

3. Correct!

4. Exactly!

5. Precisely!

6. Right.

7. Sure.

8. Totally!

9. True.

D Agreeing with a Short Phrase

1. I couldn't agree with you more!
2. I'll say!
3. I'm with you on that.
4. My feelings exactly.
5. That's a good point.
6. That's exactly what I think.
7. That's just how I see it.
8. That's just what I was thinking!
9. That's right!
10. That's so true!
11. They're ideal.
12. You can say that again!
13. You're (so) right!

E Disagreeing Politely

1. I wonder whether that's truly the case.
2. I'm inclined to disagree with that.
3. I'm not (so) sure about that.
4. I'm not so certain.
5. I'm not sure (that) it works like that.
6. Not necessarily.
7. That doesn't necessarily follow.
8. That isn't strictly true.
9. That's not necessarily true.

F Disagreeing by Giving Reasons

1. I agree up to a point; however, pencils are cheap.

2. I guess you could be right, but some research shows differently.

3. I'd agree with you if your grade proved your point.

4. I'd certainly agree if you're thinking of the summer break.

5. It's perfect for homeschool but not for class.

6. Maybe. But the problem is the weather.

7. Possibly, but your parents will have to pay for it.

8. That may be so [true], but our class is too small for that.

9. That might have been the case once, but everyone uses computers today.

10. That would be great, except that our teacher cannot speak Chinese.

11. That's a good idea, but the forecast is rain tomorrow.

12. That's a good point, but girls do not like basketball.

13. That's worth thinking about, but there is only one week left of school.

Dialogue I

Teacher: Could I ask about your camping weekend?

Student: It was wonderful.

Teacher: Where did you go?

Student: We camped next to a beautiful lake in the mountains.

Teacher: Did you see any wild animals?

Student: Yes, my father caught a rabbit, but it bit him on his hand.

Teacher: That must have hurt a lot.

Student: Absolutely! The doctor was worried about infection.

Teacher: My feelings exactly.

Student: In my view rabbits do not bite people.

Teacher: That's not necessarily true. Scared animals can be dangerous.

Student: That's a good point.

Dialogue II

Student: I went to bed at midnight.

Teacher: I strongly believe that younger students need 9 hours of sleep a night.

Student: I guess you're right, but I had to study for a test.

Teacher: In my opinion, you do not need to cram before a test if you review every day.

Student: Possibly, but I get home at nine every night.

Teacher: Wow! That is really late.

Student: Yes, I help my grandmother at her house. She has health problems.

Teacher: In that case, you did the right thing.

Student: I'm not so sure. I am so tired.

Teacher: I have reason to believe that you will pass the test with flying colors.

Student: I'm not so certain.

Unit 7

The Language of Playing Games

A Starting and Setting Up Games

1. Choose a team name.

2. Decide on your team names.

3. It's time for a game!

4. Let's play a game!

5. Tell me who is on your team.

6. Tell me your team's name.

7. What are your team names?

8. Write your team names on the board.

B Getting Started

1. Clear your desks.

2. Find a partner.

3. Find two [three / four] partners.

4. Get into pairs [groups of two, etc.]

5. Make a circle.

6. Make some room on your desk.

7. Make two lines and face each other.

8. Make two lines.

9. Put your books and pencils away.

10. This is team A (and this is team B).

11. Turn around and face away from the board.

12. You (two), work together.

C Getting the Students Ready for the Game

1. A counter can be a coin, eraser, or pen cap, for example.

2. Choose something that you can use as a counter for this game.

3. Here you are! (Here you go!)

4. Make sure there are 12 cards in your set.

5. One pack of cards for each group.

6. Pass the ball to the next person.

7. Play moves clockwise.

8. Take one piece of paper each.

9. Take one worksheet and pass the rest on to the back.

10. We play in an anticlockwise direction.

D Introducing a Dice Game

1. Choose a different counter each and place it on start.

2. If you land on this square, go back three places.

3. If you roll a 6, have another go.

4. Place your counter on start.

5. Put your counter on the first square.

6. Roll the dice and move your counter.

7. Take turns to throw the dice.

8. The player with the highest number goes first.

E Introducing a Card Game

1. Pick a card from my hand.

2. Put the cards face down on the table.

3. Put the cards face up on the desk.

4. Shuffle the cards thoroughly.

5. Take a card from the deck when it is your turn.

F Phrases During Play

1. Is it my turn?

2. It's your turn.

3. Who's next?

4. Whose turn is it?

5. You're next.

G Phrases for Quiz Games

1. Do you need a hint?

2. Does your team need more time?

3. If you get it wrong, the next team gets a chance to answer.

4. Is that your final answer?

5. You have twenty seconds to answer.

6. You only have one guess.

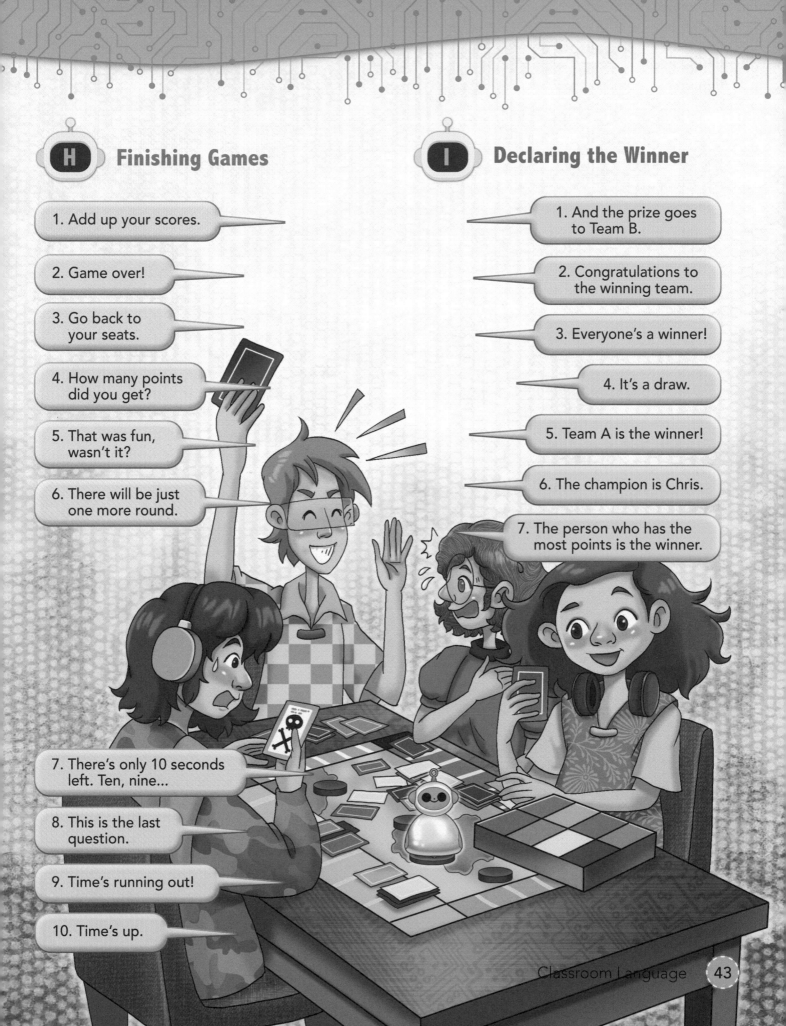

H Finishing Games

1. Add up your scores.

2. Game over!

3. Go back to your seats.

4. How many points did you get?

5. That was fun, wasn't it?

6. There will be just one more round.

7. There's only 10 seconds left. Ten, nine...

8. This is the last question.

9. Time's running out!

10. Time's up.

I Declaring the Winner

1. And the prize goes to Team B.

2. Congratulations to the winning team.

3. Everyone's a winner!

4. It's a draw.

5. Team A is the winner!

6. The champion is Chris.

7. The person who has the most points is the winner.

Dialogue I

Teacher: It's time for a game.

Student: What game are we playing today?

Teacher: I brought my dice today.

Student: What are the rules?

Teacher: We'll keep it simple today. I will ask a review question, and the team that gets it right, rolls the dice.

Student: That's easy.

Teacher: Make teams of three.

Student: Then we will have three teams.

Teacher: Now, every team, sit together at a table and face the board.

Student: We are ready for the first question.

Dialogue II

Teacher: You have ten seconds left to answer the last question.

Student: I have no clue.

Teacher: Does that mean you give up?

Student: Yes, I guess so.

Teacher: And this is the end of our game.

Student: What are we going to do now?

Teacher: Everyone, please return to your seats.

Student: Who is the winner?

Teacher: Let's add up all the points.

Student: I am sure Team Amazon won. They got many questions right.

Teacher: And the winner is ….. Amazon!

Student: Do they get a prize?

Teacher: Of course. Amazon, please come to the front to get your reward.

Student: I never win.

Teacher: Don't give up. You'll get another chance next week.

APPENDIX I

Useful Phrases to Praise Students

1. Do your best and forget the rest.
2. I am happy to see you working like that.
3. I am proud of you.
4. I believe in you.
5. I knew you could do that.
6. I love how you did that.
7. Keep moving; you are improving.
8. Keep up the good work.
9. Looking good; you are on top of it.
10. Outstanding performance.
11. That was prime classwork.
12. That's coming along nicely.
13. Way to go.
14. What an imagination!
15. You are a real trooper.
16. You are capable of amazing things.
17. You are getting better and better every day.
18. You are on fire.
19. You are on the right track now.
20. You are out of this world.
21. You blew me away.
22. You brighten my day.

APPENDIX II

Useful Rules to Keep Students Safe and Classes Manageable

A. Be Polite to Your Teacher and Classmates

1. Pay attention and be quiet when your teacher or classmate is speaking to the class.
2. Use appropriate language when speaking to your teacher or classmate.
3. Use *please* and *thank you* or *sorry* when needed.

B. Take Responsibility for Your Own Education

1. Bring all your books to school.
2. Do homework meticulously and hand it in on time.
3. Pay attention in class: That means you must take notes, participate, and ask questions.
4. Review at home every day.
5. When absent, take time to catch up on homework.

C. Keep the Classroom and Your Desk Clean

1. Do not eat during class time.
2. Do not keep food in or on the desk or in your locker overnight.
3. Make sure to put the lid or cap on your water bottle after using it.
4. Put trash into the bin at the end of every class.
5. Save our planet by put recyclables in the appropriate bin.

D. Keep the School a Safe Environment

1. Only bring scissors and cutters (exacto knives) to school when told to do so.
2. Speak to your teacher when you feel hurt or if a classmate has made you angry.

E. Use Your Communication Book Correctly

1. Complete it properly.
2. Let a parent sign it daily.

F. General School Rules

1. Do not be late for class.
2. Proceed to your classroom as soon as the bell rings.
3. Do not run in the hallways.
4. Wear appropriate clothing.
5. Stay away from the car parking.